"Ha[ve you] been vaccinated?"

Only Jesus Can Make You Whole or Clean

Mark 1:40-45

Fred Johnson

outskirts
press

Outskirts Press, Inc.
http://www.outskirtspress.com

Paperback ISBN: 978-1-9772-4409-3

Bible version is English Standard Version and King James Version.

Outskirts Press and the "OP" logo are trademarks belonging to Outskirts Press, Inc.

PRINTED IN THE UNITED STATES OF AMERICA

Dedication

Dedicated to The Blessed Trinity-One God in Three Persons The Blessed Trinity.

For me Jesus is First and foremost, "To live is Christ" (Philippians 1:21 ESV).

"Christ For Us – Our assurance
Christ With Us – Our peace
Christ In Us – Our hope of glory
Us In Christ – Our righteousness
Christ Above Us – Our sanity
Christ Under Us – Our freedom
Christ Towards Us – Our future"
-Pastor Scotty Smith

"Christ with me,
Christ before me,
Christ behind me,
Christ in me,
Christ beneath me,
Christ above me,
Christ on my right,
Christ on my left,
Christ when I lie down,
Christ when I sit down,
Christ when I arise..." - St. Patrick

Christ my righteousness, my sanctification, my joy, my hope, my strength, my peace, my everything.

To The Trinity One God in three persons blessed Trinity.

To my Christ-Centered Disciplier Pastor Allan Joseph PhD. Who I call "Papa Joseph." His Motto is "Jesus First" I am grateful to God for he sent you in my life a real bonafide believer in Jesus, Who by God's grace and desire wants to see Jesus first, in His life and ministry and you always point me to Jesus to "Christ and Him crucified." Grateful To Christ for you, always.

To my brother from another mother, Dr. Tony Marshall. He is my Trinity Seminary brother where we studied Hebrew and Greek on Campus and then went to church and praised Christ on Sunday's And Friday nights at Church. We were getting our leaning but by God's grace he was keeping us burning for Christ in The Holy Spirit.

To Pastor and Doctor Tim Keller and Doctor David Strain I am grateful to God using you both in Christ-Centered preaching, teaching, counseling that Christ has used mightily in my heart, life, teaching and preaching.

To all the Christ-Centered Gospel preachers throughout history who by God's strengthening grace lived Christ-Centered lives, prayed, preached, taught, gave counselin, worshipped Christ as The Center of it all! This book is also dedicated to you!

To my Christ-Central in Life Bible Study Fellowship member's Doctor Brenda, Doctor Jackie Copeland, Professor Paula Bunn and all those who have attended over the years. I am honored by Christ to share with you The Gospel of Christ every month for God's glory, by Christ grace and for our joy!

Table of Contents

Preface

"Have you been Vaccinated?" Only Jesus can make us whole or clean
A Leper desperately in need of a Cure

Mark 1:40-45

DURING THE TIME of an unprecedented pandemic the likes of which the world has not seen since the Spanish flu 1918-1920. This pandemic cast an incredibly great shadow of darkness, full of anxiety, grief, and death across the globe, but at the same time put a lot of things vital to life into focus, one of the major questions during the pandemic is "have you been vaccinated?" This caused me as I listened to Gospel sermons, prayed and looked to Christ in faith, to ask an even bigger question or Biblical reflection, with much deeper eternal ramifications, added, that is "Have you been vaccinated?" Only Jesus can make us clean or whole. This topic brought me to the story of the leper in Mark 1:40-45. A leper who was desperately looking to find a cure but could not find it in and of himself but Only in The Great Physician, Jesus Christ, who he bowed before in Mark 1:40. Have you bowed before Jesus as The balm, The cure, The Great Physician who is able make one clean and whole from the spiritual leprosy that is sin and has deadened your soul (Ephesians chapter 2).

God speaking through the timing of events to highlight The Ultimate Greatness of His Son Jesus as The Cure or The Balm to the sin virus

What was extremely interesting was the timing of the pandemic as it was reaching it's pinnacle, on our calendar. The timing of the peak caused an author to write during the pandemic while it was reaching its peak, the following;

> These moments of extreme pandemic are now happening in the same time or season as we mark the death of Christ, His resurrection, the remembrance of passover, the flight from Egypt, the crossing of the Red Sea This is no accident, coincidence, or by chance.

It was no accident that as we rushed for a physical vaccine, during the pandemics peak, that God was highlighting on the calendar, a Balm, The cure on The Cross from the virus of sin, on Good Friday and Resurrection Sunday 2020.

It was no accident that as The world lost over 500,000 to covid, and families were torn asunder, in grief and loss, that the savior who died and rose and ascended to The City of God, was highlighted on our calendar, during Holy Week 2020, for he had reversed the curse of sin, the virus of sin, and death by dying and rising from the grave for his select elect people.

It was no coincidence that the death and rising of Christ was being highlighted on Holy Week 2020, during the rising peak of the pandemic, to show The Ultimate Cure to the virus of sin, in Christ alone.

So "Have you been vaccinated?" Is a question that lead, and leads me to a deeper Biblical reflection to this response "Have you been Vaccinated?"Only Jesus can make you whole or clean" (Mark 1:40-45).

For The timing of all of this pandemic peaking during Holy Week 2020, was not accidentally, if with eyes of faith we see a hero of hero's is being highlighted, magnified, glorified, exhalted and upheld, from Good Friday to Resurrection Morning, over the dark clouds of the pandemic. There is a cure in Him as he sheds blood on the cross to wash away sin, on The Cross, and in His resurrection, ascension, and corination to The right hand of God. And also, now on God's right hand, Jesus is The Vaccinator of grace for every trial, every fear, every anxiety, and every pandemic.

Have you been vaccinated? Is a question that leads me to the response, and a deeper meaning than just physical vaccinations, but to a biblical response in Mark 1:40-45, "have you been vaccinated?"Only Jesus can make you whole or clean."

The Vaccine or Cure and The Vaccinator or Administer of grace

As you read this book and your not saved or you do not know Jesus as The one who has The Cure for your virus of sin or as will be addressed in the book, sin that is like leprosy, causing death, numbing, and separation from God. I prayer that Christ will save you from sin that is like leprosy. From sin's dark powerful grip of eternal death (Ephesians chapter 2). If you are saved I pray that you will see with eyes of faith, again and again and again, that Jesus rose and is seated as The Ultimate Qualified Vaccinator of grace (2 Corinthians 12:9) and he not only gives or administer grace because of His death on behalf of his chosen children on The cross, but he has graced us with himself, through his resurrection (Romans 8:11). He is with his chosen child, and in them, able to carry them through every trial, every fear, every pandemic of life. For Christ, going through The Greatest Pandemic on The Cross, taking the wrath of God on his chosen people's sin (1 John 4:10), then rising Sunday morning; means as well that if God loved me enough to meet my Greatest need at The Cross on Good Friday, can he not also meet any lesser needs for his glory and my joy.

**Have you been vaccinated? Only Jesus
can make us whole or clean.**

Mark reads 1:40

Jesus Cleanses a Leper

40 And a leper[a] came to him, imploring him, and kneeling said to him, "If you will, you can make me clean." 41 Moved with pity, he stretched out his hand and touched him and said to him, "I will; be clean." 42 And immediately the leprosy left him, and he was made clean. 43 And Jesus[b] sternly charged him and sent him away at once, 44 and said to him, "See that you say nothing to anyone, but go, show yourself to the priest and offer for your cleansing what Moses commanded, for a proof to them." 45 But he went out and began to talk freely about it, and to spread the news, so that Jesus could no longer openly enter a town, but was out in desolate places, and people were coming to him from every quarter.

The popular question today is have you been vaccinated? By Pizer, or Moderna. These COVID-19 vaccines help our bodies develop immunity to the virus that causes COVID-19 without us having to get the illness. These two vaccines have an efficacy rate of 90% or higher. Efficacy is the ability to give you the desired result of not getting the covid19 virus. But for me the bigger question is have you been vaccinated by Jesus? For Only Jesus ultimately has the cure to make us whole or clean.

Our topic is "have you been vaccinated?"
Only Jesus can make us whole or clean

In this passage, we see three shocks as the leper comes to Jesus, (David Strain, Pastor of First Presbyterian church of Jackson Mississippi, brings out three shocks, in his outline on this passage);

CHAPTER 1

The First shock was the approach of the leper.

**Look at verse chapter 1:40 And a leper[a] came
to him, imploring him, and kneeling said to him,
"If you will, you can make me clean."**

THE LEPER CAME to Jesus, but leprosy is a contagious and deadly skin disease, that covered this man and was contagious through touch. And yet He came to Jesus? During that day, the law or the CDC guidelines for a leper those days were "the leper had to be physically distance to 150 feet upwind and 6 feet down wind" (Talmud, neverthristy.org), and he had to be apart from society or quarantine himself. Sounds very familiar, in light of the pandemic, also The leper also had to cover the lower part of their face. Sounds interestingly familiar in light of the pandemic.

Coming to Jesus, the leper moved within or broke the social distancing, guidelines of the CDC of the day called the law pertaining to lepers, this was unthinkable. But there he was, no not doubt desperate, with the diagnosis of leprosy. He was desperate as he "came to Jesus, imploring him, and kneeling" and saying to Jesus, in Mark 1:40, "If you will, you can make me clean".

Leprosy a living death

A historian of the day named Josephus said "lepers were living dead men," another person said "leprosy was a living death who's healing was equivalent to being raised from the dead." And who can raise a leper from death from a sure, certain and slow death? (Edwards 69).

This man was desperate for he was a walking corpse. So desperate he kneels before for Jesus. Covered in leprosy from his head to his feet, "and yet he knelt, he knelt before The King. Have you come to Jesus? Have knelt before The King?" (Pastor David Strain).

Leprosy is an illustration of sin

Leprosy is an illustration of sin. There are many parallels between leprosy and sin, but let me give just a few (Pastor Jeff Stotttruthappliedjs. com).

Like leprosy, sin begins small. With leprosy it starts off with fatigue, tiredness, and little white dots. Isn't that how sin is? It starts off seemingly small in your life. According to James it begins with a little thing called desire.

Like leprosy, sin causes numbness. As leprosy advances you become physically numb to pain. You will burn but you can't feel the fire. You break your arm but you don't feel it. You can't feel the damage done to your body. Sin is exactly the same way. As your sin advances you don't sense the damage you are doing to yourself, to your mind, your emotions, or your relationships. You become insensitive to truth, God, and others. We become numb to the things of God.

Like leprosy, sin causes separation. If you are diagnosed with leprosy then you are removed from family and friends. Sin does the same thing. How often has sin separated a husband and wife? Parent and child? Friends? Without a doubt sin causes us all to be separated from God before we are saved and cleansed of sin (Isaiah 59:2).

Like leprosy, sin cannot be removed by law or goodness. You can't be good enough to remove sin. You can't smear the cold cream of religion on sin and hope it goes away. Just by trying to keep the ten commandments and be good and go to church does not get rid of sin. If you are lost and in your sin, the only hope for a cure a miracle… that miracle comes in the person of Jesus. **Jesus is The Cure, The grace you need.**

Like leprosy, sin causes death. If the leper is not healed and cleansed he will die a leper. The Bible says the wages of sin is death (Rom. 3:23). Sin has a wage.

Like leprosy, sin leaves a person feeling worthless and hopeless. He is away from those he loves. He no longer can do what he enjoys. His career is over. His plans for the future are over. If sin goes far enough, your life can take on a useless appearance and worthless (Pastor Jeff Stotttruthappliedjs.com).

So this man was desperate for he was a walking corpse. So desperate he kneels before for Jesus. Covered in leprosy from his head to his feet,

 And yet he knelt, he knelt before The King. Is this not what it means to be an authentic Christian. On your knees in acknowledgment of His Lordship, imploring him for the help only he can give, our desperate need, our uncleanness of soul. Only he can make us clean" (David Strain's sermon, Contagious Holiness).

"I have a great need, but I have a great Christ for my need" (Spurgeon). Have we come to Jesus? Have we come to Him to acknowledged; Our helplessness and Jesus All-sufficiency.

Our powerlessness to cure ourselves and that Jesus is All powerful and that He is able do exceedingly above what we ask or think. Our desperation and that Jesus alone can make us clean, as The Great Physician.

"Have we done this, have we knelt before him, have we come to him," for only Jesus can make us clean or whole (Pastor David Strain.)

"If Christ was not all to this leper, he would not have been nothing to him. For Jesus will never go into a relationship as part Savior or partly heal" (Spurgeon). Jesus is the Great physician to this leper. "For Jesus is God and He is everything and if he be not everything he could not be anything to this leper" (Spurgeon). Jesus completely heals this leper and Jesus completely saves.

In regards to the pandemic I know there was talk about the efficacy of some of the vaccines globally. At One point a Mayor in a city in America did not want a certain vaccine that came to his city because he was not content with the efficacy number. But when it comes to Jesus he is not a partial savior he saves completely. And as we see with this Leper, Jesus will make him completely whole or clean.

"Have you been vaccinated?" Only Jesus can make us whole or clean as a complete Savior from sin which is illustrative of leprosy.

Have we acknowledged that we have a great illness of eternal spiritual proportions beyond our ability to make ourselves well or whole. Have we acknowledged with the Leper, Christ as The Great Physician is capable of bringing the cure for our great need, that only He can bring.

Leprosy can not be cured cosmetically

The tendency is to cover up sin which is illustrative of leprosy cosmetically with self-help ideas like "you go girl,' 'Just do it,' 'let's go,' 're-invent yourself,' 'pull yourself up by your own strength,'" or our good works. But these self-help phrases are symptomatic of the fact that the spiritual leprosy of sin has numbed us to the reality we can not cure or save ourselves. No more than The leper could cure himself. The Leper needed Jesus The Great Physician. "Our sin condition is incurable by are own cosmetic efforts and good works" (Dr. Allen Joseph). The scriptures state "He that covers his sin shall not proper; but the one who confesses and forsakes them will obtain mercy" Proverbs 28:13. We like the leper do not need a life-coach, or a self-fufillment guru, or revival, we like him need a resurrection, a miracle from God. He needed Jesus The Resurrection and The Life! (John 11:25). The Balm of Gilead.

And when we are truly and indeed saved by Jesus it is a miracle we are saved! As the song writer said "saved by His grace divine, saved by new life sublime, life is so sweet and my joy is complete because I am saved, saved, saved. It's a miracle we are saved for "what manner of loved God has bestowed on us that we should be called the children of God" (I John 3:1) . . . we were like the leper for leprosy is like sin.

Like Leprosy sin caused us to be numb toward God

Like Leprosy sin caused us to be separate from God

Like Leprosy sin caused us to feel worthless and hopeless (Pastor Jeff Stottruthappliedjs.com)

Like Leprosy sin caused us to be the walking dead totally incapable of sensing God.

But It is a miracle if we are truly saved! By Christ The Great Physician!

So this leper kneels desperately before Christ to be healed, "have you knelt before Jesus? Have you come to him to say with the leper 'if you will you can make me clean'" (Pastor David Strain) Mark 1:40. Only Jesus can make us whole or clean.

How do you receive this vaccine or The cure? Is there no balm in Gilead, is there no physician there?

Jeremiah said "Is there no balm in Gilead, is there no physician there?" But Jeremiah was with a rebellious people in Judah who refused to repent from there sins and return to God. Jeremiah cries in desperation "is there no balm in Gilead? Is there no physician there?" Why then has the health of my poor people not been restored (Jeremiah 8:20)

"You know the balm in Gilead was an ointment used effectively by the people of Israel to help the healing of wounds physically. Gilead was known for this ointment or balm, because it came from a type of tree which existed in abundance throughout the region. When people are alone, facing crisis after crisis in desperation they cry 'where is God?' But The Great Physician is always near but people refuse to receive the only medicine that can help them. Is there no balm in Gilead? Is there no physician there? Yes, there is a balm in Gilead, and yes there are many Physicians there. Why then is there no healing for the wounds, the reason the spiritual wounds of people refuse to be healed is because people refuse to heed the call of God to humble themselves and receive the balm, the vaccine, the ointment from the physician. And there are many wounds of a spiritual nature that God's desires to heal but have we humbled ourselves before Him, The Great physician. Have we come to Him to be made whole? (Dr. Claude Mariottini)

I know there was reports when covid19 came out that many people said I do not need a vaccine this is not real and it ended up costing them their life. Can you imagine being sick and having the balm and the physician available but the person refuses to be made whole to have their wounds healed, by having the doctor apply the cure of the vaccine to make them whole.

Some say I do not need a vaccine. I will be just fine. But for this leper to say that in Jesus day would be unimaginable for this leper could not cure himself. He was a walking corpse.

How do you receive the vaccine?

Do you see in the text that the leper is a picture of how to receive the cure from Jesus, look in Mark 1:40.

The Lepers came as a walking dead man diagnosed with leprosy and we stand before Jesus spiritually dead in trespasses and sins (Ephesians 2:1)

The Leper was drawn to Jesus as The Only Balm or Remedy for His illness. We come to Jesus drawn by God as The Only Balm or Remedy for the sickness of sin. The scriptures declare, "No one can come to me (Jesus) unless the Father who sent me draws him.(John 6:44)

We come to Jesus just as we are. Just like the leper who came to Jesus full of leprosy, we come to Jesus full of sin.

We come to Jesus with desperation. Just like the leper who approached Jesus knowing that Jesus was his last hope, we come to Jesus knowing He is are only hope. We come to Jesus as our one and only hope because only Jesus can make us clean or whole.

We come to Jesus with humility. Just like the leper who knelt before Jesus, we kneel our lives before Jesus acknowledging that He is Lord.

We come to Jesus with respect. Just like the leper who said, "If you are willing..." indicating that he knew Jesus was in charged and believing Jesus could do something for him, we come to Jesus with respect knowing that He is in charge. Like the leper we don't demand, we ask in humility.

We come to Jesus with trust. The leper (heard about Jesus) and knew or believed Jesus could heal him. He came to Jesus with faith, confidence, and sureness of what Jesus could do. Do you believe that Jesus can cleanse you of your sin? Do you believe that Jesus is bigger and more powerful than anything you bring to Him? Just like the leper who knew Jesus could heal him and cleanse him, we come to Jesus (drawn by God, John 6:44) knowing He can forgive us and cleanse us of our sin (Pastor Jeff Stott truthappliedjs.com).

Let me say it once again so we see this powerful picture clearly, that the Leper came as a walking dead man, before Jesus, diagnosed with leprosy, and we stand before Jesus spiritually dead in trespasses and sins (Ephesians 2:1). Jesus is our only hope for a resurrection or for a cure! Have you been vaccinated? Only Jesus can make us whole. "Jesus is bigger and more powerful than anything you bring to Him" (Pastor Jeff Stott).

"Faith is only as strong as the object it is placed in"

J Gresham Machen. And "Jesus is bigger and more powerful than anything you bring to Him" (Pastor Stott). Jesus is Greater! So The leper knew he was covered with leprosy, was numb, and without feeling in his body, and he knew his condition was a death sentence. And yet he comes to Jesus who can clean Him and make him whole, For "Jesus is bigger," greater than and more powerful "than anything you bring to Him" (Pastor Stott).

Jesus said "Those that are well have need no physician but those that are sick" (Mark 9:12 ESV). Are you spiritually sick? Have you come to Him, Jesus can make you whole. Have you been vaccinated? Only Jesus can make us whole or make us clean.

So "the first shock was the lepers approach" (David Strain). This answers the question "how do you receive the vaccine?" but there is a second shock in is this passage, "the second shock is that Jesus touched the leper."(David Strain).

CHAPTER 2

The Second Shock: Jesus touches The leper

Mark 1:41 reads "moved with compassion (pity) Jesus stretched out his hand and touched him and said to him "I will be clean."

BUT JESUS TOUCHED him and said I will be clean.

By touching him Jesus was willing to touch the untouchable,

Jesus can touch the untouchable areas that no one else can touch

We have untouchable areas in our life, in our heart, in our soul, in our mind, no one can touch that area in our life, it is untouchable, but Jesus can touch the untouchable arears that no one else can touch, Jesus has the cure or remedy that no one else has a balm for. We all recall when covid19 broke out nobody had a vaccine for it, all the science labs began vaccination trials, "operation warp speed," as there was no known cure at the time.

But Jesus chosen child has no spiritual ill that Jesus can not touch and cure.

I know we had a lot of losses in the pandemic. Many crying out inside "Can anybody identify with my loss, all my pain, all my suffering, and all my losses."

Can anybody identify? Nobody can know fully and completely know your pain. They may have a taste of your experience of what your going through. A taste of your losses because they have had losses and pain and grief. But they can not know fully and exhaustively. But there is One that can, Oh! Yes there is one, God lost His Son in the darkness of The cross. As Christ took the judgment for the sins of his people, crying "My God, My God why have you forsaken me? (Matthew 27:46), That God's chosen children may never be forsaken from God, from God's presence. God knows what it means to lose the apple of His eye at The cross, in the darkness of divine judgement. He knows what it is like to lose his Son to Judgement because His Son was bearing our sin, on The cross. God The father knows what it is like to lose His one and unique Son. So where others may have a taste of losing a loved one, God knows fully so he can provide the unlimited grace, and unending mercy that only He can give.

You will never exhaust The Merciful Touch of Jesus

Only God knows eternally and exhaustively your pain, and suffering, your losses and He can provide the spiritual aide that is needed by his compassionate touch. There is unlimited mercy, grace, and power from God's hand. You will never as a chosen child of God be able to exhaust Christ. You will never exhaust the merciful touch of Jesus. "You will never limit Jesus" (Dr. Allen Joseph). Dear select elect child of God you will never exhaust his love, his peace, his mercies that are new every morning, you will never exhaust his power. You will never exhaust Jesus. So never be satisfied with just a little Jesus.

"Let the roots of God's word run deep into the good soil Of your heart until those roots grab hold of Jesus, and let The roots of God's word in your heart go deep." (David Strain's message "The Parable of The Sower"). Let the roots get rapped up and tied up in Jesus. "And Jesus will sustain you he will bring you through all things for the Glory of God. For you will never exhaust Jesus and he will always sustain you" (Dr. Strain's sermon The Parable of The Sower).

You have no Spiritual Ill to which God does not have the cure

Only God knows fully your loss and pain and is able to meet your need. We have great needs but a great God who can meet every one of those needs, regardless of the pandemics we experience.

So when it comes to God, you have no spiritual illness to which God does not have the cure.

The unsaved have the need of being cured from the sickness of sin. The saved have spiritual ills that only Jesus can restore and cure.

Also,

"by touching the leper and saying 'I will be clean' Jesus is saying 'I am willing to become unclean that you may be clean' In this regard, Jesus touching the untouchable leper and making him clean, is this not a picture of The cross. Is this not 2 Cor. 5:21 'He became sin who knew no sin that we may become the righteousness of God in Christ' (David Strain's message "Contagious Holiness").

Christ takes the robes of wickedness or the sickness of sin, that you may wear his cloths of righteousness, and be made whole.

This is a Great exchange:

For How is Jesus able to cure this leper, ultimately?

Because at the cross he would trade places with the leper.

The leper was isolated, and Jesus was cosmically isolated on The Cross, alienated from God. The leper cried "unclean, unclean," proclaiming shame, Jesus cried my God, My God why have you forsaken me? (Matthew 27:46) bearing the wrath of God on this lepers sin.

The leper was isolated from all but Jesus was isolated and alienated from God on The cross that this leper may have a home or access to God.

The leper has an illness no one could cure it was a death sentence, But Jesus took the ultimate death sentence of God's judgement on sin at The cross, so this man may have eternal life. Jesus was able to heal this man for ultimately he traded places with this man, this leper, on The cross.

So Jesus touches the man and says "I am willing be clean."

You may be worried often that no one can touch the untouchable areas in your life. And people have written you off as untouchable, you are an untouchable, you have written yourself off that I can not be cured in this spiritual area of my life. You may have given up hope of a cure in that area of your spiritual life.

But Jesus becomes untouchable at the cross, crying "my God my God why have you forsaken me?"(Matthew 27:46). Untouchable, he becomes untouchable by God, bearing our sin, that God would be able to touched us, that God would be able to touch us, and embraced us. Reflect on this, where no one else is able to touch us, and make us whole, where no one else can make us whole, but God in His powerful, compassionate touch is able to make us whole. Have you come to him? Have you knelt down before Him so he can do what we could never do in and of ourselves or no one else can do for us, make us whole, makes us clean in his Holy presence.

Jesus said at the beginning of His ministry, Jesus declared;

18 "The Spirit of the Lord is upon me,

because he has anointed me

to proclaim good news to the poor.

He has sent me to proclaim liberty to the captives

and recovering of sight to the blind,

to set at liberty those who are oppressed,

(Luke 4:18-19 English Standard Version).

At the Cross, Jesus becomes a curse that we maybe blessed. Jesus becomes untouchable bearing sin that we may become touchable by God's hand and made whole and clean.

So The leper with his mouth covered with a mask, in order not to be contagious, broke the CDC guidelines of the day or the law pertaining to lepers to approach out of desperation Jesus to be healed, but Jesus broke the CDC guidelines of the day or the law pertaining to lepers by touching the leper, the untouchable, out of compassion to make him whole. Do you need to be made? Has The Great Physician showed you your great need to be made whole?

I know the question today is have you been vaccinated? by Pizer, by Modnera, but to me there is a bigger question. Have you been vaccinated from that which we can not cure in and of ourselves? From that sin virus from which there is no man made cure. It takes The God-Man Jesus. The Great Physician. Have you been vaccinated by The Great Physician from the spiritual illness of sin? Only Jesus can make us whole or clean.

So "the second shock is the touch of Jesus, but The third shock is the command of Jesus," (Pastor David Strain's).

CHAPTER 3

The Third shock is The command of Jesus

43 And Jesus[b] sternly charged him and sent him away at once, 44 and said to him, "See that you say nothing to anyone, but go, show yourself to the priest and offer for your cleansing what Moses commanded, for a proof to them."

BUT JESUS TOLD him not to tell anyone,

But vs 45 he went out and began to talk freely about it and to spread the news, (vs 45) Jesus wanted him to keep quite.

"Jesus does not want persons who merely seek miracles. I know it's innate in us to want miracles, but Jesus wants followers who seek Him! He does not want people to come to Him to get what they want. He wants people to come to Him to get Him!" (David Strain's Message "Contagious Holiness").

Jesus wants people to come to Him for Him.

I recall woman saying that guy is after me just for what I have externally not who I really am, inside. Men say that woman wants me for what I have in my bank account or my possessions, or my position or title. The glory of being with someone who has this or that, they really do not want me for me. Nobody wants to be just networked for the connections they have, or for what they have. They want to be loved for who they are. Likewise Jesus does not want to be networked. He wants to be loved and adored for who He is not for what he gives.

"So Jesus tells him to not say anything to anyone. For Jesus He wants people to come to Him to get Him!

But Jesus dose tell him to go to the priest and offer for your cleansing what Moses commanded for a proof to them" (Pastor David Strain).

What The Law could not do, Jesus did.

"Basically Jesus is saying go show the priest that what the law could not do I could, What the law could not do Jesus did. The law had no mechanism to deal with his condition, but Jesus could deal with him. The law shut me out showing that I was unclean, but Grace or Christ welcomed me, and cleansed me. The law shows us like a mirror our leprosy, but has no mechanism for cleansing the leprosy of sin," (Pastor David Strain).

But grace is a balm, a cure for our spiritual ill.

Law vs Grace:

The Law Commands vs Grace or Christ Beseeches
The Law Judges vs Christ makes us blameless on The Cross.

15

The Law produces wrath vs Christ is Our Peace
The Law defeats us vs Christ who is Our Victor
The Law exposes our lack vs Christ is Our completeness
The Law demands Righteousness vs Christ is Our righteousness
The Law Kills vs Christ is Our Resurrection and Our Life.
The Law faded in Glory vs Christ is Our glory
The Law strengthens sin vs Christ is Our Strength
The Law can not perfect vs Christ is Our Perfection
The Law enslaves vs Christ liberates
(Shorewood Bible Church, Rolling Meadows, IL).

"The law tells you what to do, but it can't give you the power to do it. Jesus tells you what to do, and he gives you the power to do it" (Pastor David Strain) through and by His Holy Spirit. "I can do all things through Christ who strengthens me. (Philippians 4:13) Christ ultimately strengthens me with resurrection power (Philippians 3:10).

"Jesus came to do what the law could not do . . .
Is this not romans 8:3 'For what the law could not do, in that it was weak through the flesh, God sending his own Son in the likeness of sinful flesh, and for sin, condemned sin in the flesh. . .' .So Jesus tells the leper go show yourself to the priest for what the law could not do Jesus did!" (Pastor David Strain).

So Jesus directs the leper to go show yourself to the priest as a proof. That only Jesus, reflect on this, only Jesus, can do that which the law could never do.

Story from Bible School

In bible school two students Shane and Carson were talking about this passage and Shane a student said "wow after the leper was cleaned by Jesus, he could not contain his praise to tell all that Jesus had done."

Shane said "if I was him I would have went out to praise Jesus for all he had done for me. I could go hug my family members and friends in the community, who I could not be around. I would go get a burger at McDonalds and go to Hillary's ribs. I could feel things I could not feel before. I could go places I never could go and see things I never could see." The other student, named Carson, who was very sharp and quick on his feet said "I need to let you know Shane, you were that leper." Shane, got it! Oh he said "wow, snap, that's right Carson there was no way I could cure myself from the spiritual leprosy of sin, my goodness was not good enough, as sin covered me from head to toe, through out my soul, heart, and through out my very being, and then Jesus came and only He could make me clean, Only Jesus can make me whole."

You were that Leper

And I have come by to tell you, today, I need to tell you something that will be eternally vital for your spiritual resurrection and spiritual healing, you we were that leper,

We were that leper covered with leprosy, like sin, and we could not heal ourselves.

We were that leper desperate to be free from a living death, for we were dead in trespasses and sin (Ephesians 2).

We were that leper that was quarantined from God, eternally distant from God, alienated from God until Christ found us. It was not the leper who found Jesus, it was Jesus who found the leper.

"In this is love, not that we have loved God but that he loved us and sent his Son to be the propitiation (wrath absorber) for our sins" 1 John 4:10.

We were that leper, But Jesus The Great Physician came, He touched you and I and in compassion and said "I am willing be cleaned." **The Physician became the patient on the cross taking our spiritual sin sickness to make us whole.**

"I looked at my hands and they looked new and I looked at my feet and they did too" (gospel song).

The song writer said "I looked at my hands and they looked new and I looked at my feet and they did two (George Jones)." The scriptures says "If any man be in Christ he is a new creature. . .". A new creature, in which Christ lives within by his Holy spirit, a new creature where Christ is our righteousness, a new creature where Christ is our sanctification, a new creature where Christ is our Perfection, a new creature where Christ is our Completeness, a new creature where Christ is our Balm, and our Cure, and a new creature where Christ is our Grace, a new Creature where Christ is our Savior and King.

Why was Jesus able to cure us?

The answer is The cross, Jesus took our place on The cross as our substitute.

He climbed on the hospital bed called the cross, bearing the ultimate spiritual illness of sin, that we may be made whole. Have you come to Jesus? Have you been vaccinated? Only Jesus, Only Jesus Now he can make you whole.

He became isolated and alienated from God that we may be received into the presence of God.

He loss His face in the darkness of The cross, bearing the judgement for our sin, that we may have a face before God.

He lost his name, at the cross, bearing our judgement, that we may have a new name before God, written in the Lambs book of life, written in Glory (Luke 10:20).

"Oh what manner of love God should bestow on us that we should be called the children of God" (1 John 3), That we should be called children of God, it's a miracle we are saved and made new and whole.

He became a curse on a tree that we may be blessed. Galatians 3:13

says; "Christ redeemed us from the curse of the law by becoming a curse for us—for it is written, 'Cursed is everyone who is hanged on a tree.' "

Have you been vaccinated? Only Jesus can make you whole or clean.

There was a Great exchange on The Cross, Jesus for us.

For Jesus was willing to be broken that you and I maybe made whole.

"Jesus The greatest insider becomes The greatest outsider on The Cross" that God's select elect children "who were outsiders, sinners, may become insiders and behold the face of God" (Pastor Paul Kim, Redeemer Church San Diego).

This is a Great exchange:

Christ exchanges our spiritual poverty for his spiritual riches, our wickedness for his righteousness, our rejection for his perfection, our sickness for his wholeness.

Why was Jesus able to cure the leper, you and I? Because he took our, place on the Cross. This was a great exchange "He became sin who knew no sin that we may become the righteousness of God in Christ" (2 Corinthians 5:21). For we were that leper ultimately that needed The healing restoring touch of The Savior to make us whole, to make us clean.

Only The Precious Blood of Jesus can make us whole or clean

Pastor Alistarr Begg expresses How precious The blood of Christ to cleanse us from sin and make us whole;

Precious Blood!

…The precious blood of Christ.

1 Peter 1:19

Standing at the foot of the cross, we see hands and feet and side all distilling crimson streams of "precious blood." It is "precious" because of its redeeming and atoning efficacy. By it the sins of Christ's people are atoned for; they are redeemed from under the law; they are reconciled to God, made one with Him.

Christ's blood is also "precious" in its cleansing power; it cleanses from all sin. "Though your sins are like scarlet, they shall be as white as snow."1 Through Jesus' blood there is not a spot left upon any believer; no wrinkle nor any such thing remains. O precious blood that makes us clean, removing the stains of our iniquity and permitting us to stand accepted in the Beloved despite the many ways in which we have rebelled against our God.

The blood of Christ is also "precious" in its preserving power. We are safe from the destroying angel under the sprinkled blood. Remember, it is God's seeing the blood that is the true reason for our being spared. Here is comfort for us when the eye of faith is dim, for God's eye is still the same. The blood of Christ is "precious" also in its sanctifying influence.

The same blood that justifies by taking away sin also quickens the new nature and leads it onward to subdue sin and to obey the commands of God. There is no greater motive for holiness than that which streams from the veins of Jesus. And "precious," unspeakably precious, is this blood because it has an overcoming power. It is written, "And they have conquered him by the blood of the Lamb."2 How could they do otherwise? He who fights with the precious blood of Jesus fights with a weapon that cannot know defeat.

The blood of Jesus! Sin dies at its presence; death ceases to be death: Heaven's gates are opened. The blood of Jesus! We shall march on, conquering and to conquer, so long as we can trust its power!(1) Isaiah 1:18 and (2) Revelation 12:11 (Truth of Life Devotional by Pastor Alistair Begg).

Have you been vaccinated? Only Jesus
can make us whole or clean.

The song writer expressed it well "what can wash away my sin nothing but he blood of Jesus? What can make me whole or again? Nothing but the blood of Jesus, Oh precious is the flow that makes my sin as white as snow. No other fount I know, nothing but the blood of Jesus" (Robert Lowery).

CHAPTER 4

Lastly, How do you know you have been fully vaccinated? Where Jesus makes you whole or clean

WELL AS I reflected on the physically process of vaccination, in San Diego, California, at the health center, this caused me to see, how this process pointed ultimately to The greatest story, The story of Christ, The gospel story.

First, when I arrived there was a short line, and I made it through quickly, and signed my name and provided my driver license card as ID. Second, The Doctor greeted me with saying "I am Doctor Amaza, which arm would you like to receive the shot." She had on a white coat with her name tag, that said Doctor Amaza on it, recently I saw a badge that said "vaccinator" on it. Doctor Amaza was a qualified vaccinator. Next she sanitized and cleaned her hands and put on gloves before vaccinating me.

Let me just pause for a minute to say:

Jesus is Qualified as The ultimate Vaccinator for He does not need, sanitation liquid or gloves for his hands, for Only Jesus hands are Holy, Only Jesus heart is pure and Holy, Only His life is spotless (Isaiah 6:1 following; Hebrews 7:25-26).

Jesus is Qualified as The ultimate Vaccinator for He is The High Priest for God's chosen people, He that ascended into the heavens. . . and he is able to sympathize with our weaknesses, he is one who in every respect has been tempted as we are, yet without sin (Hebrews 4:15).

As The Ultimate Sympathizer of our weaknesses, He is able to give mercy and grace at His throne (Hebrews 4:14-16). Jesus is qualified to administer grace, for only His grace is sufficient, He said "my grace is sufficient for you, for my power is made perfect in weakness" (2 Corinthians 12:9). Christ grace is sufficient for every trial, every struggle, every heart break, every weakness, every pandemic.

The ultimate Mediator between God and Man is The Ultimate Qualified Vaccinator

For Jesus is qualified as The ultimate Vaccinator. For He alone is the only mediator between God and man, the man Christ Jesus. The scripture declares, "For there is one God, and there is one mediator between God and men, the man Christ Jesus"(1 Timothy 2:5). And the greatest intervention between God and man, is The God-Man, Jesus.

.Let me say briefly:

Only he can intervene to give the cure we needed, the wholeness we needed, the grace we needed, the mercy we needed, the spiritual strength we need, and the ultimate joy we needed. Do you need an intervention? Jesus is The ultimate qualified vaccinator and interventionist as The Only Mediator between God and Man. Only His grace is sufficient! And only His Mercies are new every morning, great is his faithfulness.

Jesus is Qualified as The Ultimate Vaccinator also because He is The Ultimate Wounded Healer:

He embraced all our wounds on The cross that we maybe healed.

The Ultimate Wounded Healer:

I had a co-worker once not in my current state of California. I will call her Sheila. Sheila showed me a picture in her office of a Mexican women, deep in Mexico, holding a Bible in a green field with mountains in the background. The women had a white dress on a beautiful day. The picture was so peaceful and so calm. Some Americans came to share Bible stories with the people of this village and to assist them with food and care, because it was a area in great need. But Sheila told me shortly after that picture was taken, the next day at this location, a helicopter flew in and military men dismounted from the helicopters and start shooting the people of the village. It was a massacre. Several in the village lives where taken. Sheila was abused in several ways, her life was not taken but she felt like her life was taken and lost forever. Sheila said she came back to the United States, and told her story to carrying friends over and over and over again, for many years. She shared it with counselors, but many of the counselors did not work because she said "talking engaged the frontal part of my brain, but could not impact the trauma, that was buried in the back of my brain." But she said after telling her story of trauma, again and again, for many years, she said "I accepted my story." She said once she accepted her story, she told me "my capacity or ability to be with others suffering expanded tremendously or greatly." She now ministers to those in crisis in the emergency room of a hospital.

And when she said I told my story again, and again to friends until I accepted it. And it increased my capacity or ability to be with others and now she is a wounded healer with people in crisis.

When she said this, it made me think of Christ accepting God's will to go to the cross, to drink of the cup of God's wrath on his people sin. And, Christ suffered so greatly on the cross that his suffering capacity expanded to the deepest depths and the highest heights, and widest width, as he absorbed God's wrath on the cross, for his elect child's sins. No one's capacity to suffer was expanded greater than The Christ on the cross. Christ suffering was the greatest in every way. So now Christ can be with anyone who is suffering, like no other. He is The Ultimate Wounded Healer, who can empathize with suffering on every point, on every level, like none other.

1 Corinthians 13:7 says "Love bears all things, believes all things, hopes all things, endures all things. Love never never fails." Love is personified in this verse because Love is a person. Jesus it that love.

And Jesus can give, and administer the grace you need. For he bore it all, suffered, and endured it all on that cross.

Do you worry deep in your heart who can bear the guilt, the weight of my suffering, and trials. Who can understand the suffocating worries and strangling anxieties, that are crushing my soul?

Jesus said "Come to me all, who labor and are heavy laden and I will give you rest" (Matthew 11:28-30). The Bible says "casting all your cares on him for he cares for you" (I Peter 5:7).

At the cross the Christ capacity to suffer expanded to the highest heights and deepest depths, the widest width, so he can be with his elect child in any type of suffering. Whatever suffering in the heart, the mind, the soul, or the spirit. Christ is able to administer grace. He is able to vaccinate grace, because he was touched with the feeling of our infirmities in every way (Hebrews 4:15). He's been there, done that, without sinning. Because He was wounded on an infinite level, on a cosmic lever or The highest level on The cross for us, so He can heal spiritually on any level! He is qualified as The Ultimate Vaccinator for He is The Ultimate Wounded Healer.

Our problem at this point is not the vaccine but finding qualified vaccinators

President Biden said at one point during the pandemic "Our problem is not the vaccine but finding qualified vaccinators." And as I reflected on it, I am so glad that Jesus, The Only Mediator between God and Man, is able to administer the unending supply of grace, the unending supply of mercy to our greatest need. Jesus is Qualified as The ultimate Vaccinator because He is The Ultimate Wounded Healer in the life of his chosen child.

Jesus is both The Grace and The Administer of Grace

Grace is a person for scripture says "For the grace of God has appeared, bringing salvation. . . "Titus 2:11. And Jesus is The grace of God that has appeared. God graces us with himself, and grace is also administered by Jesus for the scriptures says "My grace is sufficient for thee my grace is made perfect in your weakness"

II Corinthians 12. Jesus is The Ultimate Qualified Vaccinator for He both graces us with himself as a person and He also, administers the grace that is sufficient for all our needs. And Christ grace is sufficient for every trial, every struggle, every heart break, every weakness, all spiritual ills of his people.

The Physical Vaccination Process Points to The Greatest Story

Going back, to the physical vaccination process, located, in San Diego, After, my physical vaccine, was given, by Doctor Amaza, she sent me to a waiting room for 15 minutes, to be observed, to see if there were any side effects, to the vaccination, and thank God, I was ok.

Then I was directed outside, to a table, where a man said "Here is your card that you have been vaccinated, keep it with you," in other words "hear is your receipt, of vaccination."

"Here are your receipts
The debt of sin has been paid in full"

As I thought about it, the medical person saying "here is your card or proof of vaccination" or basically "here are your receipts of vaccination." Months later I heard a message by Pastor Milton Bowden, called "here are your receipts," The debt of sin has been paid in full. As I heard the message and received several insights, and I added to the message and changed the message to fit this message.

"Here is your receipt" because at the cross, Jesus was paying my sin debt it was a bloody transaction as he said "it is finished" (John 19:30) in the Greek, the word is "te-tel-stai" meaning "paid in full." That is te-telstai was written, on receipts during new testament times. Indicating on the receipt the item was "paid in full."(The Greek-English lexicon by Moulton and Milligan page 630).

I owed a debt before The Holy God I could never pay, and Jesus paid a debt he did not owe, when He said on The Cross "It is finished."

From time to time when I return an item to Target, or Walmart they always ask do you have the receipt to show the item was purchased or paid in full. I say "yes I do."

Let me say briefly: I am not about to return any of the spiritual blessings, or promises Christ purchased at the cross for they are unreturnable for the true child of God.

Well How do I know I have been fully vaccinated? Only Jesus can make us whole or clean for He gave a receipt at the cross, "it is finished" my sin debt, before The Holy God is paid, It was paid in full. Consider it crimson currency, consider it a bloody signature, at the cross, "it is finished."

Sin is described in scripture as a personality (Romans 6:12), "Let no sin reign . ."Sin is pictured as a ruling King. Also sin is pictured as animal In Genesis 4:7 it says ". . . sin is crouching at your door; it desires to have you. . . ". So when sin like a personality a ruining king or a animal comes after you or through a personality, or person, comes toward me to tempt me or seduce me away from my Christ, my King, The Love I have longed for all my life, Jesus, "I say no, no, no, I have already received the balm, the ointment of his grace has already been broken open on The cross and applied, I have already been, redeemed, from your power,

Here is my receipt," it is a bloody signature, from The cross, I have been washed in the blood of The lamb. Jesus said "It is finished."

This bond, this power you once had over me, sin, it is over

(Romans 6), it is done, because at The Cross, your power has been broken, the chains shattered, when Jesus paid my sin debt, here are your receipts. Because of The cross you have loss your claim on me that is Sin described as a personality, like an animal ready to pounce in scriptures has no right to put his hands on me, I belong to The King. " Whom The Son (Jesus) has set free is free indeed" (John 8:36).

The scriptures also declare "God has delivered his people from the domain of darkness and transferred them to the kingdom of his beloved Son" Colossians 1:13. So when sin comes to pull me or wants to lure me away from my Christ, I proclaim or preach, Here is your receipts! I am no longer bond to your power sin or I am no longer condemned, or a slave to you sin, any longer. I am no longer a slave but a son of God through Christ, "There is therefore now no condemnation to those who are in Christ Jesus" (Romans 8). My savior paid the debt on the cross. The scripture declares to the church;

"By canceling the record of debt that stood against us with its legal demands. This he set aside, nailing it to the cross. He disarmed the rulers and authorities and put them to open shame by triumphing over them in him"(Colossians 2:15-16). Jesus has paid The record of debt in full!

The balm, the ointment has been applied, the cure has been broken open at The Cross, the cure applied to my sin sick soul, it is finished, I have been set free, redeemed by The blood of The Lamb. Jesus said "It is finished" it is paid in full, here is the receipts. I am free, sin, from you're your command, your control, your domineering force or power, through the heroic bloody sacrifice of Christ, my King.

The song writer said "Jesus paid it all, all to him I owe sin had left a crimson stain but Jesus washed it as white and snow."

Another song writer said "there is power, power, wonder working power in the Blood of The Lamb."

And yes there is the ultimate power, in Christ, His bloody sacrifice, and bloody signature at the cross, to break the bondage, to cut loose the ties, to free from chains, and the domain of sin, paying the sin debt in full.

A song writers, Charlie D. Tillman, expressed

Jesus breaks every fetter (a chain, manacle, shackles, to restrain a prisoner placed around the ankles). Jesus breaks every fetter, I will never doubt my Savior [three times], For He cleanses me [chorus]

I will rest on His promise [three times] which is given me.

I will shout Hallelujah [three times] For He sets me free.

Yes Jesus, breaks every chain! At the cross and his resurrection!

And, I am just as free as my savior, for the scriptures declare to the church; "But God . . . raised us up with him and seated us with him in the heavenly places in Christ Jesus" (Ephesians 2:6). I am just as free as my savior, for Hebrews 12 says "But you have come to Mount Zion and to the city of the living God, (by faith). . . to a myrid of angles in festal garb." I am free because, he was bound on the tree and crucified for me for me, that I would be free from sin's power and penalty. I am free because he took my ultimate penalty on The Cross.

I still have battles but that is because
Jesus won the war at The Cross

I still have battles with indwelling sin but that is only Because Jesus won The ultimate war at The cross paying my sin debt. I still have battles until heaven, until glorification, with indwelling sin, but that is merely guerilla warfare because The ultimate War has been won at the cross. Christ banner over me of Love came at the cost of heroic bloody sacrifice, stating "It is finished." Now I have been redeemed. Yet I battle and I fight with "the sword of the spirit,"(Ephesians chapter 6), and "praying in the spirit or praying the word, or The gospel." But this battle is only because, Jesus won The war at Calvary, from sin's domain, and sin's power.

So when the temptation or tempter comes with every sort and kind of sin, to lure me, and wants to pull me, away into this sin or that sin, we are called to stand on the infalliable Word of God, which is without error, The

Truth, proclaiming, "whom the Son has set free is free indeed" (John 8:36). So sin "you have no dominion here, you have no power here," Jesus said "it is finished," that is the bloody signature, that is the receipt and here are your receipts. I am no longer bound. I am no longer held bound by your sway and control or dominion.

Revelations 12 says "they (believers) overcame the evil one by the blood of the lamb and the word of their testimony" (bearing witness, to what Christ did on the cross on the believers behalf, Revelations 12:11).

Jesus said on The Cross "It is finished," that is sins' debt is paid in full, Only Jesus' crimson currency and bloody signature could set me free. The scriptures state "let the redeemed of The Lord say so whom he has redeemed from the Hand of the enemy" Psalms 107:2.

Isaiah 53:4&5 says "Surely he hath borne our griefs, and carried our sorrows, yet we did esteem him stricken, smitten of God, and afflicted. 5 But he was wounded for our transgressions, he was bruised for our iniquities, the chastisement of our peace was upon him; and with his stripes we are healed."

1 Peter 2:24 says, He himself bore our sins in his body on the tree, that we might die to sin and live to righteousness. By his wounds you have been healed. ". . .By His Stripes we are healed" (Isaiah 53:5b).

We were healed from the power of sin and the penalty of sin.

How do I know I have been fully vaccinated? It is Only Jesus that can make us whole or clean. Jesus said "it is finished" The sin debt is paid in full. Here are the receipts and to any tempter or desire that attempts to bring you into bondage or captivity, stand on the truth and proclaim, "here are the receipts of my freedom." Jesus The king has granted, me, immunity, dying, in my place, on The cross, and paying for my sins, I have been set free! Only The King, Jesus can grant immunity because he took my place and paid my sin debt, in my place. The sin debt is signed with the bloody signature of The King!

The song writer said;

Jesus paid it all

All to him I owe

Sin had left a crimson stain

He washed it white as snow

Jesus paid it all, all to him I owe,. . .

now, Jesus Indeed, I find Thy power, and thine alone,

Came and changed the lepers spots

And it melt the heart of stone

Jesus paid it all!

So I do not have to yield to the temptations any more. Christ redeemed me from the curse of the law by becoming a curse for me. Christ brought me out of the bondage and slavery of sin. I have been set free. Tempter here are your receipts, I have been set free! You have been served, if you will, the divorce decree is in, as the old romance with you sin is over, it's over, Through Christ my King, who provided freedom, from you power and penalty and in glory your presence, Here are your receipts, that it's over. It is over!

The young people say "by Felicia"

Young people would say or have a saying "by Felicia," and here she is representative of sin, and a relationships time that has expired, and come to and end, it is over. Who is your Felicia? In scripture she is similar too that Jezebel lady in Revelations 2:20 seductively leading church members away from Christ into idolatry. Whatever, whoever that personality of sin is in your life, point Felicia to the cross for she represents the old sin (Romans 6:12, as sin is described a personality), she represents the Jezebel alluring others away from Christ to idolatry (Revelations 2:20), and let Felicia know it is over, it's over, it finished, this thing between you and me is over. Felicia is representing the old sin, and the old romance, and it is over, her seductive ways, her manipulation, her deceit, her cunning allurements, her enticements to ensnare, her entrapments into addictions, and her seductive ways of pulling you away from Christ your First love, it's all over, "By Felicia." God has offered me someone eternally better in Jesus. I found ultimate healing, and freedom, through my savior's heroic bloody death, on my behalf, on The Cross. "By Felicia" say what you will, it's over, I found joy in Jesus, hope in Jesus, peace in Jesus, grace in Jesus, eternal love, eternal spiritual strength in Jesus. My Ultimate balm and cure, is in Jesus. Jesus is my savior, my King and has set me free from you, "it is finished." "if Christ reigns in my heart, there will be no space for another reigning power" (C.H. Spurgeon). So it's over with any false reigning personalities; for by God's grace and strength and power, through His Word, Jesus The reigning King of my heart is first!

How do you know you have been vaccinated? Only Jesus can make one whole or clean. Jesus my savior said "it is finished" By His stripes I am healed from sins' power, and sins' condemnation, from sins' penalty. Here are your receipts, my saviors "it is finished" on The Cross, this thing between you and sin, is over, it is over, it is all over! At Christ Cross, where my ultimate Love, died for me, and made His chosen child, His own, His bride.

So when the tempter comes, point sin, and point temptation, to the cross, point them, to the risen saviors' nailed scared hands, and preach to them here are your receipts. Jesus said "it is finished!" The nail prints show he has paid the sin debt in full and has risen victoriously over sin, hell, death, and the grave, Here are your receipts! The nail prints of His victory, this means, No more bondage for me, no more captivity for me as Christ bride!

For I once owed a debt I could never ever pay,

But Jesus, paid a debt He did not owe.

Christ transaction on The Cross was a bloody Transaction:

It secured everything we needed; it is the receipt for all the promises and blessings of God. "All the promises of God in Christ are "yes" and Amen"
2 Corinthians 1:20.

Everything that we know and appreciate and praise God for in all Christian Experience both in this life and in the life to come springs from this bloody cross. Do we have the gift of the Spirit? Secured by Christ on the cross. Do we enjoy the fellowship of saints? Secured by Christ on the cross. Does he give us comfort in life and death? Secured by Christ on the cross. Does he watch over us faithfully, providentially, graciously, and covenantly? Secured by Christ on the cross. Do we have hope of a heaven to come? Secure by Christ on The Cross. Do we anticipate resurrection bodies on the last day? Secured by Christ on the cross. Is there a new heaven and a new earth, the home of righteousness? Secured by Christ on the cross" DA Carson.

The promise "The gates of Hell will not prevail against . . ." the church (Matthew 16:18 ESV). The church is secured in the blood of The Lamb.
The promise "Greater is He that is in me than he that is in the world" secured in the blood of The Lamb.
The promise "No weapon formed against me shall prosper" is secured in the blood of The Lamb."
All Praise be to God that Christ transaction on The Cross was a bloody Transaction,
And Secured everything, the chosen child of God, needed; it is the receipt for all the promises and blessings of God. "All the promises of God in Christ are "yes and Amen." All The promises are secured in the

blood of The Lamb!

So any worries in your mind, any anxieties in your soul, any temptations attempting to lure you away as the chosen beloved Child of God, from our first Love, Christ, preach the gospel to yourself, and every personality trying to come in between us and Christ our First love, point them to the cross, point them to the nailed scared hands and wounded side of Jesus, and proclaim, Here our your receipts, for, Jesus said "it is finished" this thing between you and I is over, I have been cured from sins sickness, by the blood, the balm, the cure, provided by My savior, and Great Physician! Believe in Him, trust Him, rest in him, depend on Jesus, for his finished work on your behalf on The cross! Walk by faith and not by sight, Looking to Jesus!

Nail Prints of Victory

Lastly in John 20:24–28 It reads,

24 Now Thomas, one of the twelve, called the Twin was not with them when Jesus came

(after Jesus resurrection). 25 So the other disciples told him, "We have seen the Lord." But he said to them, "Unless I see in his hands the mark of the nails, and place my finger into the mark of the nails, and place my hand into his side, I will never believe."

26 Eight days later, his disciples were inside again, and Thomas was with them. Although the doors were locked, Jesus came and stood among them and said, "Peace be with you." 27 Then he said to Thomas, "Put your finger here, and see my hands; and put out your hand, and place it in my side. Do not disbelieve, but believe." 28 Thomas answered him, "My Lord and my God!" (John 20:24-28).

Thomas known as doubting, Thomas, was not present when Jesus first appeared to His disciples, in His resurrection body. The disciples told Thomas, Jesus is risen and Thomas said "I will not believe until I put my finger in his side." In other word's it was like saying "show me the receipts" (Bowden). Well Jesus appeared to the disciples with Thomas present this time, and told Thomas go ahead and put your finger in my side. Jesus said do not disbelieve, but believe. Thomas said 'My Lord and my God!' (Gospel of John chapter 20).

Jesus is Lord, for as Savior, on the cross, he paid the sin debt for his chosen people, He rose, and appears to Thomas to say look, it is me, look at the nail prints in my hands, look at the gash in my side, in other words, it is like saying, here are your receipts that sins' power Is broken, here are your receipts, that sin debt is paid for, here are the receipts that "every promise of God in Christ is yes and Amen." Here are the receipts that redemption from sin is secured through my blood, here are the receipts, no more power to the bondage of sin and it's domain, it over, Here are the receipts that death has died, and heavens gates are open to the redeemed. Here are the receipts ". . .all the promises of God find their Yes in him" (2 Corinthians 1:20). In Jesus! "Every promises of God in Christ is yes and amen." "It Is finished!"

Trust Christ, rely on Christ, depend on Christ, The cure, has been given, The balm has been broken open at The Cross, and applied, The redemption has been achieved, the captive have been set free! For Jesus says Look Thomas at my hands, the nail prints are there, look at my feet and my side, the spear gash is there, look Thomas here and here and here, it is I, Jesus, look at the nail prints, here are your receipts! That the cure has been given through my blood! The balm broken open at The cross to make you whole or clean! And whom The Son has set free is free indeed!

Have you been vaccinated?
Only Jesus has the cure to make us whole or clean.

Appendix: Reflective Questions for Individuals and Groups

Chapter One: "The First shock is The approach of The Leper" (Dr. Strain).

1. How is Leprosy an illustration of sin?

2. What are the ways sin like leprosy is being covered up?

3. Fill in the blank Dr. Allen Joseph says "our sin condition is incurable by are own _____ _____ and by _____ _____. Discuss and reflect on this in your group.

4. How do you receive the vaccine?

Chapter Two: "The Second shock is The Touch of Jesus" (Dr. Strain).

1. Why can God touch the untouchable areas in our life?

2. How is Jesus able to cure the leper Ultimately?

3. Fill in the blank at the cross Jesus becomes _____ that we may be _____.

4. How did the leper break the CDC guidelines of the day or the laws according to Lepers?

5. How did Jesus break the CDC guidelines of the day of the law pertaining to Lepers?

Chapter Three: "The Third shock is The command of Jesus" (Dr. Strain).

1. Why did Jesus tell the leper go and show yourself to the Priest?

2. Why did Jesus tell the leper not to tell anyone what Jesus had done for him?

3. Can you name some of the contrast between The Law vs Grace?

4. Fill in the blank The Physician became the _____ on The Cross taking our _____ _____ _____ to make us _____.

5. In the story from the Bible School what did Carson reveal to Shane?

6. In what ways is the leper in story a picture of us?

7. Fill in the blank The song writer said "I looked at my _____ and they looked new and I looked at my _____ and they did too (gospel song)."

8. Why was Jesus able to cure us from the leprosy of sin?

9. What is the Great exchange?

10: Fill in the blank Alistarr Begg says "The blood that_____ by taking away _____ also quickens the _____ _____ and leads it onward to subdue _____ and obey the _____ of God."

Chapter Four: How do you know you have been vaccinated? Where Jesus makes you whole or clean

1. Why is Jesus qualified as The Ulitmate Vaccinator?

2. Fill in the blank Jesus _____ all our _____ on The cross that we _____ _____ _____.

3. Why is Jesus The Ulitmate Wounded Healer?

(Let the group take a moment of silence and pray individually, privately and quietly. Pray to Christ identifying the wounds over your life and thanking Christ for all wounds he has healed for you by embracing them all at the cross. For Christ is The Love personfied that bore it all for his chosen children, read I Corinthin 13:7-8a. This is a private prayer moment of silence for each group individual group member not public. It their are tears it's ok to cry In the presence Christ who bore it all for his chosen children. If you have to follow up with a trusted Elder/Pastor at a Gospel believing Church please do so).

 4. What does "te-tel-stai" mean in Greek?

5. Fill in the blank "I ____ ____ I could not pay before The Holy God and _____ a _____ he did not _____.

6. What are the scriptures that show Christ has paid the sin debt of his chosen people?

7. Fill in the blank the chosen child of God was healed from the _____ of sin and the _____ of sin.

8. Take a moment of silence in your small group and quietly pray to God (if you need to confess quietly in prayer confess to God) to show you the sins that are called out in scripture adultery, fornication, pornography, lying, jealousy, envy, pride (Romans 6:11-13; I Corinthians 6:9-11) or any sin or sins that are trying to reign in your body. Pray and ask God to give you strength by The Holy Spirit and His word, to say "by to your Felicia." That is an old romance or relationship of sin attempting to lure you away from fellowship with Christ, your first Love. (If you have to get with a trusted Elder/Pastor in a Gospel Believing church to confess and hold you accountable in this area please do so.)

9. Name some of the promises in scripture secured by The blood of The Lamb!

All the answers to these questions are in the book.

Works Cited

Begg, Alistair "Precious Blood" TruthForLife Devotional.

Bowden, Milton. Sermon idea "Here are your receipts: All debts Have been Paid" Preached on April 7, 2021 on Resurrection Sunday at Temple of Grace church incorporated, San Diego, Ca.

Carson, D.A Reformed Baptist Scholar.

Gresham, Mecham, J. Reformed Scholar.

"Jesus Heals A Leper" Mark 1:40-45 Part 1 and Part 11; Pastor Jeff Stott truthappliedjs.com

Jospeh, Allen PhD. Pastor All nations christian Fellowship, Brooklyn Center, Minneapolis, MN.

Kim, Paul, Pastor, Redeemer Church, San Diego, Ca.

Talmud, Neverthristy.org.

The Greek-English lexicon, by Moulton and Milligan.

Law vs Grace Chart. Shorewood Bible Church, (posted on website by Administrator), 1900 Hicks Road, Rolling Meadows, IL 60008.

Lowery, Robert's, Hymn "What can wash away my sin?"

Mariottini, Claude. "Is there no balm in Gilead?": Dr. Claude professor of Old Testament, Northern Baptist Seminary.

Strain, David. Contagious Holiness, Sermon, Pastor at First Presbyterian church of Jackson Mississippi.

The Greek-English lexicon, by Moulton and Milligan.

"The Gospel According to Mark," The Pillar New Testament Commentary, James R. Edwards.

CPSIA information can be obtained
at www.ICGtesting.com
Printed in the USA
BVHW031126080821
613941BV00017B/379

9 781977 244093